Anonymous

The Scotchtown Memorial

Or, the centennial of the Presbyterian Church of Scotchtown, 1796-1896

Anonymous

The Scotchtown Memorial
Or, the centennial of the Presbyterian Church of Scotchtown, 1796-1896

ISBN/EAN: 9783337409463

Printed in Europe, USA, Canada, Australia, Japan

Cover: Foto ©Lupo / pixelio.de

More available books at **www.hansebooks.com**

The Scotchtown Memorial;

or,

The Centennial

of the

Presbyterian Church of Scotchtown.

1796-1896

'96 ꞏꞏꞏ E. G. Hulse, Printer, Newburgh, N. Y. ꞏꞏꞏ'96

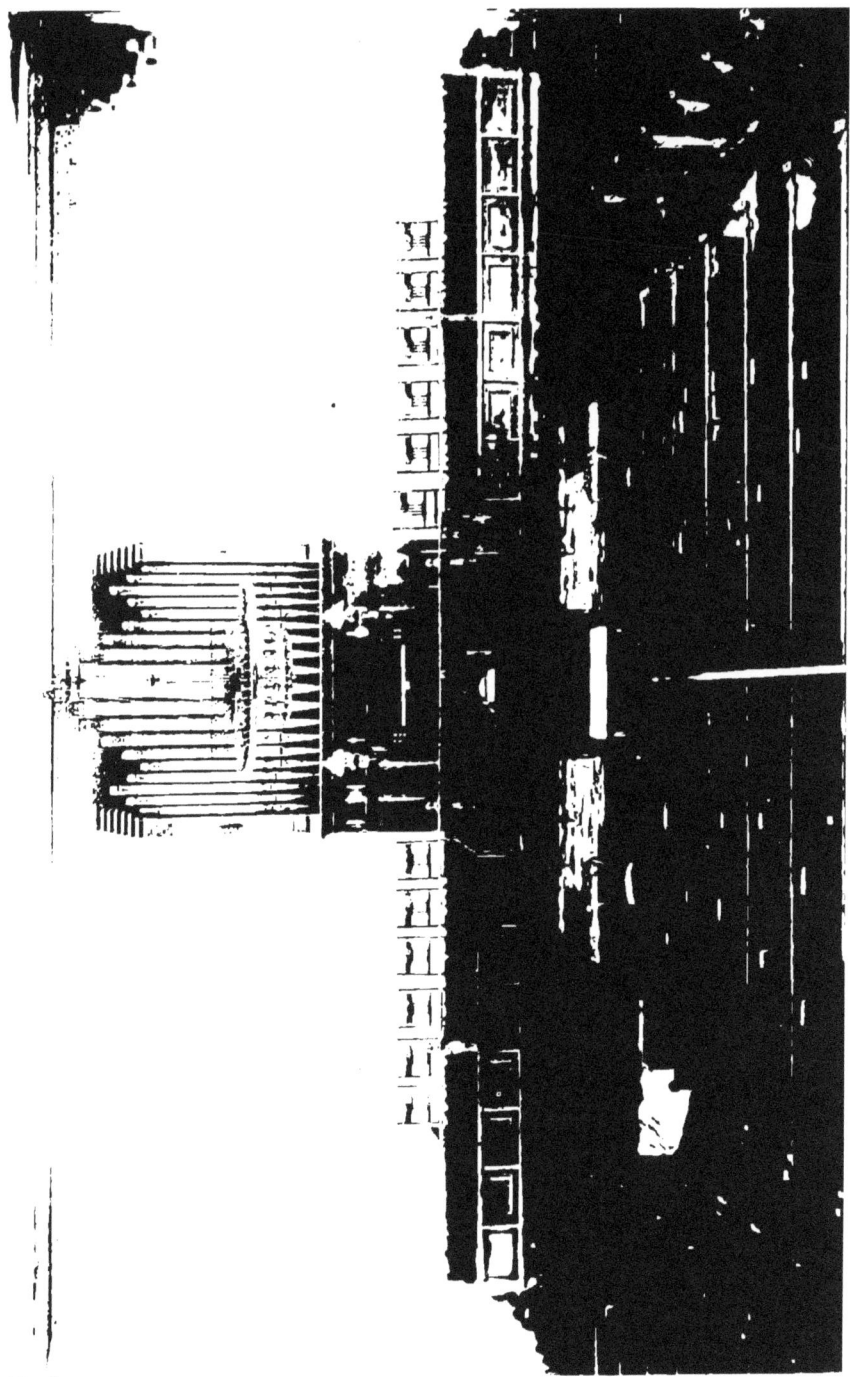

Introduction

I T is with heart-felt gratitude to the Great Head of the Church that we undertake the pleasant task before us. The existence of a church, a living church, for the period of one hundred years in one spot is reason for sincere thanksgiving unto the Most High.

The celebration held July 28th, 1896, is the centennial celebration of the organization of the Scotchtown Presbyterian Church.

We are deeply indebted to the Rev. S. W. Mills, D. D., of Port Jervis, for the historical matter contained in this little book. A difficulty has been greatly felt in the preparation of the historical address, from the fact that the early church records were burned when the home of the first pastor was destroyed by fire.

We, therefore, desire to tender our sincere thanks to all persons who have contributed items of any historical interest.

We send out this booklet with the hope that it will meet a desire which is prevalent and a want which is deeply felt.

THE COMMITTEE.

JAS. R. MANN,
Chairman.

Historical Sketch.

IN the history of the churches of the Presbytery of Hudson, prepared by the Rev. Henry A. Harlow, by the appointment of Presbytery in 1887, and receiving their approbation when completed, there is this statement regarding the church, whose centennial we are now celebrating. " The Church of Scotchtown is one of those which do not make history fast." The correctness of this statement will appear when we consider that during the one hundred years of its existence it has had but four pastors, the last of whom, the present pastor, is only upon the second year of his pastorate; that during this long period it has dissmissed but one of its ministers, and this after thirteen years of faithful and acceptable service : that their first pastor died among them after an unbroken service of forty-three years, followed by five years of great bodily infirmity, during which, though incapacitated for labor, his pastoral connection remained unbroken until severed by death; and that their third pastor began and ended his entire ministry of forty-two years with them. All this is creditable alike to minister and people. To the minister, indicating on the part of those filling this sacred office, a consciousness of the fact that " The lines had fallen to them in pleasant places " and that they have been contented with their lot doing their Master's service in the place assigned to them. Creditable to the people also as furnishing evidence that they have not had itching ears or been captivated with novelties, anxious to hear some new and strange voice, but preferring the familiar tones of their own loved shepherd in whom they have learned to confide.

The Church at Scotchtown it would seem was organized, so far as its civil or secular organization is concerned by the choice of Trustees, in January 1796. Its ecclesiastical organization by the election of elders was not effected until six years later, in June, 1803. The first movement looking toward the establishment of a church, of which we have been able to find an account, was made December 24th, 1795, when in response to a public call the inhabitants of the neighborhood met at the house of George Houston to consider the propriety of organizing a church. Previous to this all who desired to avail themselves of religious privileges were accustomed to go to Goshen or to Montgomery. By reason of the distance this was found to be very inconvenient and attended with many difficulties.

Hence the desire and effort to have religious services in their own community. Mr. Houston, at whose house the meeting was held, was a member of the Presbyterian Church of Goodwill, near Montgomery, then called the Wallkill Church. Col. William Faulkner was chairman of the meeting. It was resolved " To open a subscription for the purpose of erecting a meeting house at the corner of the roads above the house of George Houston." There being a division of sentiment among those present respecting the denomination with which the proposed organization should be connected, a resolution was offered by Jacob Mills and adopted by the meeting that it should be under the care of the Presbytery of Hudson (which had just

been constituted), connected with the General Assembly
of the Presbyterian Church. Those who favored another
connection thereupon withdrew from the meeting and subsequently assisted in organizing the Associate Reformed
Church at Bloomingburgh. A few weeks later (January,
1796), Jacob Mills, Patice Bodle, Samuel Dunning, Edward McNeil, John McCarter, Peter McLaughlin and
George Houston were chosen Trustees. George Houston
gave nearly three acres of land for a church lot and bury-
ing yard, and steps were taken as early as practicable to
erect a house of worship, Daniel Denton being engaged
to enclose and paint the building. He began work June
1st, 1797, and the frame was raised July 1st, following,
and was enclosed and painted by September 12th, 1797.
The building remained in this condition, without plaster-
ing, without pews, without pulpit and without stoves for
nine years, although occupied regularly for worship.
Temporary seats made of rough boards were used by the
hearers, and a rude platform and desk by the preacher.
The building in this condition presented a striking con-
trast to our sanctuaries of the present day, with their well
cushioned seats, attractive pulpits furnished with sofa or
easy chair, carpeted aisles, stained-glass windows, melodi-
ous organ and the entire building furnace or steam heated.
And yet it can not be doubted that as true, sincere worship
and acceptable to the Most High, was there offered as now
ascends to Him.

In September, 1806, the Trustees engaged Daniel Denton to finish the inside of the building for $515.00. The
edifice would hardly be regarded as a model of artistic
taste and beauty, either externally or internally. Externally destitute of all adornment, without blinds, cupola or

spire, there was nothing to indicate the purpose for which it was erected and to which it was devoted. Without porch, vestibule or hallway, the entire interior of the building was occupied by the auditorium, across which three aisles ran, one leading from each front door. When first built there were square box pews running around against the wall, both on the first floor and in the gallery, and in the re-modelling of the church in 1832, the square pews on the first floor were removed and seats, as at present, substituted in their place. The pulpit was placed upon the broad side of the building opposite the doors, high up from the floor and reached by a winding flight of steps eight or ten in number with doors at the top enclosing the minister securely when once within. A gallery ran around three sides of the room and in either corner of it opposite the pulpit and most remote from it a portion was partitioned off and furnished with elevated seats for the colored people, who thus occupied the highest seats in the synagogue. These portions of the edifice were for many long years well filled by colored people who came in large numbers regularly to the sanctuary. Here in this plain and unimposing structure the people of God worshipped for two generations. Here the Gospel was proclaimed in its purity and simplicity to the awakening and conversion of multitudes. Here the Holy Ghost descended repeatedly in mighty power and " Times of refreshing from the presence of the Lord " and from the glory of His power were enjoyed, so that on one occasion 96 persons stood up and confessed Christ as their Savior and entered into covenant with him. " The Lord will count when He writeth up the people that this and that one were born here."

After standing for fifty-seven years, this building was

torn down and the present edifice was erected in 1854 by Zachariah H. Luckey, of Bloomingburgh, at a contract price of $4,366.00. The Building Committee consisted of Mr. Archibald Slaughter and Mr. W. D. Hurtin. It was publicly dedicated on February 6th, 1855, the dedication sermon being preached by the Rev. J. M. Krebs, D. D., of New York City, from Luke 7 : 5. " For he loveth our nation and he hath built us a synagogue."

A few months after the first building had been raised and enclosed, Jacob Mills and George Houston appeared before the Presbytery of Hudson at a meeting held in Goshen, April 19th, 1798, as commissioners from a Presbyterian Church in the Town of Wallkill, and requested that said church be taken under the care of Presbytery and that supplies might be appointed them. Their request was granted and the Rev. Nathan Kerr of Goshen, the Rev. John Joline of Florida, and the Rev. Mr. King of Goodwill, were appointed to supply the pulpit one Sabbath each.

The Rev. Mr. Kerr preached the first sermon in the church. The following year on April 17th, 1799, John White and Patrick Bodle appeared before the Presbytery at Newburgh, as commissioners from the church and requested that the Rev. Methuselah Baldwin, should be appointed to preach in the church one-third of the time until the next stated meeting of Presbytery. Mr. Baldwin consenting to do so, their request was granted and he continued to supply the church regularly a part of the time until January, 1803. On April 4th, 1803, a call upon Mr. Baldwin was made and signed by the Trustees and attested by the Rev. Andrew King, Moderator of the meeting. This call was presented to the Presbytery by Geo.

Houston, commissioner, on April 20th, 1803, and on
the following day Mr. Baldwin signified his acceptance of
the same. On June 30th, 1803, the Presbytery met for
his installation. The installation sermon was preached
by the Rev. Mr. Freeman of Newburgh, who also gave
the charge to the people, the charge to the pastor being
given by the Rev. Mr. Kerr.

METHUSELAH BALDWIN.

The first pastor of the Church, was born in Newark,
N. J., December 15th, 1763. He was the second son of
Jeremiah and Mehetabel Baldwin by the second marriage
of his father. Jeremiah had several children by his first
marriage, and three sons and a daughter by the last. Methuselah survived all the other members of the family of
both branches. His father died when he was but twelve
years old. His mother was a most godly and judicious
woman, whose instructions had great influence in forming
the character of her son. About the age of sixteen his
religious character became decided and he thought he had
experienced a change of heart. He was then attending
upon the ministry of the Rev. Mr. Chapman, of Orange,
N. J., living about seven miles from church, which distance he walked regularly every Sabbath. Neither distance nor any other obstacle prevented his attendance.
Soon after his conversion he felt called to enter the ministry, and although many obstacles seemed to be in the way
the desire was not quenched. With no father to direct
him, and no means to prosecute a course of study, he cast
himself upon the promises of God. He entered the Acad-
emy at Orange, after engaging for the payment of his

11

board on condition of payment when he should become able. He also obtained a loan of some money which was expended before completing his college course. There were then no societies or organizations in the Church to assist needy young men desiring to enter the ministry and they were thrown upon their own resources unless aided by private hands.

He pressed on in his course amidst obstacles and discouragements until he finished his college course, graduating from Queen's College, at New Brunswick, now Rutgers, in 1789. After graduating he spent some time in teaching at Elizabeth-Town, N. J., to enable him to discharge his pecuniary obligations incurred in prosecuting his studies, which he fully accomplished, at the same time prosecuting his theological studies under the direction of the Rev. Dr. McWhorter, of Newark. He was licensed to preach by the Presbytery of New York, in October, 1791, and soon after was appointed to spend a year in missionary labor in Northern and Western New York, at that time both a natural and moral wilderness. At the close of this term he received a call from the Presbyterian Church of Pleasant Valley, Dutchess County, N. Y., which he accepted and where he was ordained and installed pastor November 6th, 1792. The Rev. Mr. Kerr presided over the meeting at the time of his ordination and installation, the Rev. Mr. King preached the sermon from Dan. 2 : 44, the Rev. Mr. Minor gave the charge to the pastor and the Rev. Mr. Close to the people. While here Mr. Baldwin was married on May 4th, 1792, to Jane Higgins, of Newark, N. J., who died soon after, leaving two infant children. After four years at Pleasant Valley, he removed to Mathersfield, in the Town of New Wind-

sor. While here he was married to Julianna Evertson.
He assisted while here in forming the Presbytery of Hudson, upon the dissolution of the Presbytery of Dutchess
County. He was the last survivor of the original members of this Presbytery (Hudson). He supplied various
vacant churches within the bounds of the newly organized
Presbytery. While at Mathersfield, in New Windsor, he
was invited to supply the Church of Scotchtown, which,
after three years, resulted in his permanent settlement as
pastor, as already stated. The congregation at that time
was small and feeble, unable to support a minister properly
and hence he purchased a farm, on which he lived until
his death, the same having been occupied for many years
by the late George Wallace, and where his family still reside. While living here the dwelling house of Mr. Baldwin was twice consumed by fire, in one of which the records of the Church, prior to 1825, were destroyed, the loss
of which has been felt in the preparation of this historical
sketch.

On the day of Mr. Baldwin's installation the following
persons were chosen elders in the church, thus completing its ecclesiastical organization: John White, Peter McLaughlin, David R. Arnell and George Houston. Before
the time for ordination Peter McLaughlin died, when
Ephraim Everett, Adam Millspaugh and Enos Ayres were
chosen, and all six were ordained on June 16th, 1804. The
first report to Presbytery, in 1805, gave the numbers as
forty-four. Mr. Baldwin's labors were greatly blessed and
under his ministry the membership of the Church increased
largely. Several extensive revivals were experienced during his pastorate. The first marked season of religious
interest was in 1815, and which extended to other churches

in the vicinity. It commenced in the summer season in what was called the upper neighborhood and continued through the harvest until fall. It has been estimated that more than one thousand persons were added to the various churches in the county that summer. Again in 1819 or 1820, in 1830 and in 1836. In 1830 ninety-six persons were received at one time upon profession of their faith.

Mr. Baldwin was a man of great kindness and benevolence of heart, greatly beloved by his people for his many excellent qualities, as well as for his labors in seeking to promote their spiritual welfare. While receiving a meagre remuneration for his services, he seems to have been contented with it, making it evident to his people that he sought not theirs but themselves.

He was a man of great prudence and discretion as appears in the judicious treatment of many perplexing difficulties that came up during his ministry for adjudication. He was faithful and zealous in the discharge of his duties as pastor, watching over the flock committed to his care with great tenderness and fidelity, and his labors were greatly blessed in its enlargement and increase, and in the ingathering of large numbers into the church. Goldsmith's description of the village pastor in his " Deserted Village," portrays most admiringly the character of the first pastor of this Church, so far as we understand it,

"A man he was to all the country dear,
And passing rich with forty pounds a year.
Remote from towns he ran a goodly race
Nor e'er had changed nor wished to change his place.
To relieve the wretched was his pride,
And e'en his feelings leaned to virtue's side.
But in his duty prompt at every call
He watched and wept, he prayed and felt for all.
At church with meek and unaffected grace.
His looks adorned the venerable place:
Truth from his lips prevailed with double sway
And fools who came to scoff remained to pray."

14

His multiplied and arduous labors during an extensive revival in 1836, with all the anxiety and sense of responsibility attending such a state of things proved too great a tax upon his strength, which together with his advanced years disqualified him for prosecuting his work and led to securing a colleague. In the fall of 1838, he was laid aside from his labors and only preached two or three times afterwards. His last sermon was preached from II Tim. 4 : 6–8. " For I am now ready to be offered and the time of my departure is at hand. I have fought a good fight. I have finished my course, I have kept the faith ; henceforth there is laid up for me a crown of righteousness which the Lord the righteous judge shall give me at that day."

" His last years were those of great bodily weakness and infirmity, of humble submission and confiding trust and of patient waiting for the glory to be revealed. His confidence and trust in the blood of atonement as the only ground of acceptance with God, were firm and unwavering, accompanied with a sense of personal unworthiness and of the utter worthlessness of all his own doings, every act of his life being, as he said, tainted with sin, and no one to be regarded with complacency. He had long ceased to take a lively interest in the world and his spirit was ripening day by day for the heavenly world." *

The state of his mind in view of his departure was well indicated in the passage chosen by him for his funeral sermon. " I have waited for thy Salvation O Lord." His death occurred February 27th, 1847, in his eighty-fourth year.

* Funeral Sermon by Rev. E. D. G. Prime.

REV. EDWARD DORR GRIFFIN PRIME

The second pastor received a call from the church Mar. 21st 1839, at first as co-pastor, with the Rev. Mr. Baldwin, and after his death he was the sole pastor. He was born at Cambridge, Washington Co., N. Y., November 2d, 1814, and was the son of the Rev. Dr. Nathaniel S. Prime. He was graduated from Union College in 1832, taking the Latin oration, one of the honors of the institution. After teaching three years he entered the Theological Seminary at Princeton in 1835, and was graduated from it in 1838. He was licensed to preach by the Presbytery of North River, and a few months after began his labors here. His ordination as collegiate pastor took place July 12th, 1839, the sermon being preached by his father, Rev. Dr. N. S. Prime, from II Cor. 6 : 10. " As poor, yet making many rich."

He married first Maria D. Wilson of Princeton, N. J. Some years after her death, and after leaving Scotchtown, he married Eliza Goodell, daughter of Rev. Dr. William Goodell, missionary in Turkey. In the fall of 1850 he went to New Orleans on account of the health of his wife, where he supplied one of the Presbyterian Churches of that city during the winter, and on his return in May, Mrs. Prime died while on the journey home.

In December 24th, 1851, he resigned his charge here on account of lung trouble and went to Augusta, Georga. He then took charge of the Presbyterian Church in East 86th Street, New York City, for a year. After that he spent the year 1854–'55 in Rome, as Chaplain of the Embassy, under the appointment of the American and Foreign Christian Union. In October, 1855, he returned to New

York and became a regular editor of the New York Observer, which he had served for some months in 1853 while his brother, Samuel Irenaeus Prime, the regular editor, was in Europe. His death occurred the seventh of April, 1891.

The church was favored in procuring the services of Mr. Prime, afterwards known as Dr. Prime, as colleague for Mr. Baldwin, and subsequently their pastor for many years. His mild and amiable disposition, his uniform courtesy and agreeable manners, the attention shown by him to all classes alike and his faithfulness in the discharge of pastoral duty greatly endeared him to the people. Modest and unobtrusive he was yet firm and decided in his convictions and when the occasion called for it did not hesitate to express them. Possessing good natural abilities and his mind thoroughly trained, his sermons were prepared with care and were full of instruction and very profitable to his hearers. His ministry was full of blessing to the church and his departure matter of general regret among the people. In the Summer of 1850 a large number (48) professed conversion and united with the church upon profession of their faith in Christ. During his pastorate here he wrote, at the suggestion of his brother Irenaeus, a series of letters for the New York Observer entitled "Letters from the Country," signed Eusebius, describing some scenes in his pastoral experience. One or two of these we recall. One was, as we recal the caption "The triumphs of grace or the two sisters," showing how differently the spirit of God operated in the conversion of two sisters. The other was an account of a funeral upon the outskirts of his congregation to which the writer of this sketch accompanied him. The deceased

was a poor man living remote from the highway and access to whose cabin was only reached by a narrow path over which no wagon could pass. After the services the coffin was suspended from a pole borne upon the shoulders of two men and thus carried to the highway and placed in a wagon to be taken to the place of interment. The preparation of this series of letters showed him to hold the hand of a ready writer and we have long suspected had something to do with his at length occupying the editorial chair. After the departure of the Rev. Dr. Prime the church was vacant for about ten months when a call was made upon the

REV. DAVID BEATTIE

who became its third pastor. He was the son of William Beattie and Sarah Belknap and was born at St. Andrews, Orange County, N. Y., Dec. 27th, 1828. His college course was passed at Union College and his theological course at Princeton Seminary. He was licensed to preach by the Presbytery of New York and was ordained to the ministry and installed pastor of this church Nov. 4th, 1852. The opening prayer was offered by the Rev. John Johnston, of Newburgh, and the prayer of ordination by the Rev. John H. Leggett. The sermon was preached by the Rev. Dr. W. D. Snodgrass from John 18: 34. The constitutional questions were proposed by the Rev. D. N. Freeland, the charge to the pastor was delivered by his brother, the Rev. Dr. R. H. Beattie, and that to the people by their former pastor, the Rev. Dr. E. D. G. Prime. His death occurred June 19th, 1894, in the sixty-sixth year of his age and the forty-second of his pastorate over the church, his pastorate extending over about the same length of time with the active ministry in the church of the Rev. Mr. Baldwin. In 1853 he married Isabella Cumming. After her death he married N. Jennie Comfort. The greatest revival during his pastorate occurred in 1869, when over one hundred professed their faith in Christ as their Saviour.

Mr. Beattie's departure has been so recent, comparatively, he was so well known to all here present and so highly esteemed that but little need here be said concerning him. As in the case of his predecessor we can say that the church was favored in securing so faithful and devoted a pastor, one so well qualified in every way to take the spiritual oversight of the flock. Having a well balanced mind, well trained by education, and stored with information ; a most acceptable preacher : of sound judgment ; frank, open and undisguised in manner, as indicated by his frank and open countenance ; familiar and free in his intercourse with his people ; often found at their homes and especially in seasons of trial and affliction, sympathizing with them in their every trouble and imparting advice and counsel as needed ; giving his ministrations to all classes alike, rich and poor, high and low, he won his way to the hearts of all and gained a hold upon them which could never be broken. His labors were abundant and unremitting in season and out of season for forty-two years, until his work was finished and the summons came from the Master to " Come up higher."

The fourth and present pastor, the

REV. JAMES R. MANN

was born in Northumberland County, in the Province of Ontario, Canada, on September 27th, 1861, being the son of Alexander Mann and Elizabeth Thompson. His col-

legiate studies were pursued at University College, Toronto, Canada, where he obtained honors throughout his entire college course in the department of mental and moral philosophy. His first year in theology was pursued in Knox Seminary, Toronto, and his second and third year's theology in Princeton Seminary, N. J., graduating at Princeton in the class of '91. He was licensed to preach the Gospel by the Presbytery of New Brunswick, N. J., and was ordained to the ministry by the Presbytery of Lehigh, October 7th, 1891. On the same date he was installed as pastor of the Presbyterian Church, Ashland, Pa., having supplied said church since June of the same year. Those taking part in the ordination and installation exercises, were the Rev. Jacob Belville, D. D., Rev. A. M. Woods, Rev. J. N. Elliott and Rev. H. W. Tolson. He was married on December 29th, 1892, to Jessie E. Haig, daughter of David Haig and Margaret McDonald. His call to become pastor of this church was made December 26th, 1894, and his installation took place May 7th, 1895, at which time the sermon was preached by the Rev. R. H. McCready, Ph. D., the pastor was charged by the Rev. Chas. Beattie, D. D., and the people by the Rev. J. C. Forsythe. The Rev. Dr. Freeman, offered prayer and the Rev. Jas. A. McGowan, presided.

The imperfect sketch of the history of the church thus presented, suggests a few reflections.

1. *We should hold in grateful remembrance its first founders.* Those who plant the institutions of religion in a new community are deserving of all honor and praise. It is like opening fountains in a desert where refreshing streams shall gladden and revivify coming generations.

The first settlers here were, to a considerable extent, of Scotch extraction and hence the name given to the place. These and others of different nationalities were God fearing men who prized religious privileges and embraced an early opportunity to secure them. To this end they gave of their scanty means, made sacrifices and self-denials, endured discomfort, sitting upon bare, hard board benches in a cold, unwarmed building in mid-winter, that they might worship God and bring up their families under religious influences. We have reaped the fruit of their toil and sacrifice. They labored in their day and generation and we have entered into their labors.

2. *The preservation of the church in its uninterrupted enjoyment of religious privileges through all these years calls for devout thankfulness.* The continued existence of a church in the world, composed of imperfectly sanctified human beings often differing from one another in matters of church policy and doctrine and often holding their differences with great tenacity, coming in collision too as it must from the very object of its organization with the corrupt passions and prejudices of sinful men, is indeed a wonder of wonders. Such an organization having, as in the present instance, an unbroken existence for one hundred years, kept alive not by state aid or vested funds but by the voluntary contributions of the people; which has been the rallying place for the people of the surrounding country regularly once a week; where religious services have been held without interruption generation after generation except now and then a Sabbath at rare intervals, such an organization is an object of profound interest and regard. A light that has shone for a century in the same

place without having been once extinguished and that still sends out its illuminating beams; a fountain from which during this period have issued refreshing streams and whose waters still flow in crystal purity; a tree that has borne fruit for successive generations and that still fails not, all these are regarded with deepest interest. And so we look upon a church whose long existence in a community has been a fountain of perennial blessing refreshing thirsty souls, a light guiding wandering ones and pointing them heavenward, a tree whose fruit is as manna from heaven nourishing to immortal life.

The preservation of this church in its unbroken existence during an entire century, calls for devout thankfulness to the Great Head of the church. As the fathers have passed away, the children have risen up to take their places, so that we see now in the session a lineal descendant in the third generation of one of its earliest elders.

3. There is cause for gratitude in the *spirit of harmony that has prevailed in the church in all its long history.* It has never been rent by factions, nor agitated with strife and contention, but has been the abode of peace. Of the people who have worshiped here, it can be said, " Behold, how good and how pleasant a thing it is for brethren to dwell together in unity." There have been matters at times pertaining to the interests of the church, concerning which honest differences of opinion have been held, but its peace and prosperity have not been disturbed thereby. In everything affecting its welfare, there has been through its entire history unusual agreement, a disposition to yield individual opinion to the common good of the whole congregation. In the great disruption of the Pres-

byterian Church in 1837, with all the exciting scenes connected therewith, even rendering in many instances individual churches asunder, this church remained united and undisturbed by the strife. The most serious disturbance or disagreement in its whole history probably was in the effort to secure a successor to the Rev. Mr. Prime. At one time it assumed a threatening aspect, alienating temporarily kindred and near friends, though happily not to a very great extent. All this soon disappeared upon the settlement of the Rev. Mr. Beattie, to which his prudent and judicious course as pastor greatly tended.

4. Another matter calling for thankfulness is found *in the frequent seasons of spiritual refreshing enjoyed by the church.* It has had many extensive and powerful revivals during its existence. These are the glory of the church and intimately connected with its prosperity and increase. There were several of these of great power and extent during the ministry of the first pastor. In some instances the whole surrounding country was moved thereby as the trees of the wood are moved by the wind, and this too at a time when Evangelists and Revivalists were scarcely known and when the chief instruments were the pastors themselves, assisted, as occasion called for it, by neighboring ministers. Other seasons of religious interest have been enjoyed since under the succeeding ministers.

5. As a last item we mention *those who from this church have entered the ministry.* The number of those either reared in the bosom of the church or whose names have been on its roll of members who have given themselves to the work of preaching the Gospel either at home or

Rev Ralph Bull formerly of Westla— N. Y. omitted.

23

abroad is ~~seven~~ *Eight*. We give their names in the order of their entering the ministry and their places of labor as far as ascertained.

1. John II. Morrison went as a missionary to India in 1838 and was connected with the station at Allahabad and was among the earliest missionaries of the Presbyterian Board. His wife died of cholera at Calcutta, April, 1838, on his way to his field of labor. On account of his fearlessness he was known as the " Lion of the Punjaub, " and yet in personal intercourse he was affable and genial and thoroughly devoted to his work. The " Week of Prayer " now so universally observed by Christians of every name the world over is said to have originated with him. After the great Sepoy rebellion in 1857 he moved the Lodiana Mission to call upon all Christendom to observe an annual week of prayer for the conversion of the world. In 1863, while on a visit to this country, he was chosen Moderator of the General Assembly at its annual meeting at Peoria, Illinois. His death occurred at Dehra, India, September 16th. 1881. He has two sons and a daughter (Mrs. Dr. Thackwell) in the mission work in India.

2. Samuel G. Weeks, while teaching here united with the church and entered on a course of study preparatory to the ministry. graduating from Princeton College in 1838, and from the Seminary there in 1842. He was stated supply of the Presbyterian Church at Leonidas, Michigan, in 1842–'43 : of the church at Haw Patch, Ind., in 1843–'44 : and of the churches of Wolf Lake, Haw Patch, and Warsaw, 1844–'46. He died at Wolf Lake, Ind., May 21st, 1846.

3. Samuel W. Mills graduated from Rutgers College in 1838, and from the Theological Seminary at New Brunswick in 1842. Was pastor of the Reformed Church in Bloomingburgh from 1842 to 1858, and of the Reformed Church in Port Jervis from 1858 to 1872.

4. Arthur Harlow graduated at Union College in 1858. Entering Princeton Seminary in 1860, and graduating in 1863. He was pastor of the 2d Presbyterian Church at Washingtonville from 1863 to 1871. Died near Goshen, June 19th, 1873.

5. Patrick L. Cardon, after completing his College and Seminary studies, went to Siam as a missionary, after laboring there for some time he returned to America and was pastor of the Presbyterian Church in Manteno, Ill., in 1871, and for a few years subsequently. After that he served as stated supply for several years at Marysville, Cal., and from 1887 until his death, in 1890, he served the church at Red Bluff, Cal.

6. T. Cumming Beattie, son of Rev. David Beattie, was a graduate of Princeton Seminary, and was ordained and installed pastor of the Presbyterian Church at Chester, by the Presbytery of Hudson, on June 27th, 1882. At the present time and since 1890, he has been pastor of the Presbyterian Church, Albuquerque, New Mexico. He also served the church at Las Animas, Col., as stated supply from 1888 to 1890.

7. James A. McWilliams graduated from Union Theological Seminary, N. Y., May, 1885, and was ordained by

the Presbytery of Hudson and installed pastor of the Presbyterian Church in Port Jervis in 1885, and is at the present time pastor of the Presbyterian Church in Sing Sing. Four of the above have ceased from their labors while the remaining three are present to-day and participating in these interesting exercises.

In addition to the foregoing, there was a Mr. Calderack, a laboring man, an enthusiastic member of the Christian Endeavor Society of this church, who attended Mr. Simpson's Missionary school in New York City, and was sent out to Africa under the care of his school as a Missionary, although not ordained. His death occurred a year or two since.

9. Rev Emmet Sloat. formerly of this Church was a Student in 1896.

List of Trustees of Scotchtown Church.

Jacob Mills, 1796,
Samuel Dunning, 1796,
Edward McNeal, 1796,
John McCarter, 1796,
George Houston, 1796,
Gilbert Roberts, 1801,
John Tears, 1803,
Luther Smith, 1811,
Moses Bull, Jr., 1817,
Jason Corwin, 1823,
John McWilliams, 1828,
Samuel Roe, 1833,
James McWilliams, 1834,
John White, Jr., 1835,
Geo. S. McWilliams, 1838,
Selah R. Mapes, 1840,
Abner Bull, 1844,
George Goldsmith, 1845,
Charles B. Connor, 1849,
James H. Harlow, 1851,
William D. Hurtin, 1852,
Edmund S. Mills, 1854,
Harvey McMonagle, 1856,
George Wallace, 1857,
Henry Puff, 1859,
William N. Coleman, 1861,
David E. Houstin, 1863,
Harvey Roe, 1865,
Charles McWilliams, 1868,
Alfred Mills, 1870,
Joel Brown, 1872,
J. F. Myers, 1873,
Moses B. Miller, 1874,
Thomas A. Mills, 1880,

Patrick Bodle, 1796,
Moses Phillips, 1796,
Samuel Brunson, 1796,
Peter McLaughlin, 1796,
John White, 1798,
Jas. S. Miller, 1802,
Geo. W. Vail, 1808,
Seth Williamson, 1813,
Stephen Harlow, 1820,
Jacob Mills, Jr., 1825,
Ferdinand Bailey, 1833,
Samuel Bull, Jr., 1834,
Oliver Bailey, 1834,
Moses Goldsmith, 1836,
William Wallace, 1840,
Charles Mills, 1843,
Archibald Slaughter, 1844,
Stephen Harlow, Jr., 1848,
Alanson Slaughter, 1851,
James F. Boak, 1851,
Gabriel Myers, 1853,
Braddock Decker, 1855,
Thomas Youngs, 1856,
Asher Beattie, 1858,
John H. McWilliams, 1861,
John E. Brewster, 1862,
Lewis Brewster, 1865,
William N. Clark, 1868,
Alexander Sloat, 1869,
Edwin Mills, 1871,
Daniel R. Clark, 1872,
Wm. Augustus Robbins, 1873,
David B. Myers, 1878,
David Redfield, 1882,

Samuel M. Slaughter, 1883,   Harvey McWilliams, 1885,
J. Monroe Brown, 1885.   Wellington Harlow, 1886.
Abner Mills, 1886.   William H. Puff, 1887.
James Houstin. 1889,   J. E. Boak, 1889,
J. D. Mills, 1891,   Jesse Bull, 1891,
Dr. A. C. Santee, 1892,   J. Ed. Miller, 1892,
            Herbert Mills, 1895.

The First Pew Holders in the First Church.

George Houston,
Daniel Comfort.
John White,
David R. Arnell.
Gabriel N. Philips,
Jas. S. Miller,
Daniel Bailey,
William Philips,
Mrs. Wm. Brown,
Enos Smith.
Jacob Mills,
Adam Millspaugh,
Samuel Brunson,
Heirs of Thomas Watkins.
Isaac Witter,
Peter Puff. Jr.,
Ezekiel Roe,
Moses Bull. Jr.,
Archibald Streau,
Ephraim Everett,
Johaunis Young,
Daniel Hasbrook,
Luther Smith,
John McWilliams,
Mrs. Gilbert Brown,
Moses Philips,
Felix Randall,

Daniel and Jas. Sloan,
Patrick Bodle,
James Clark,
John Savage,
David Miller.
Jane Tuthill,
Alexander Corey,
Rev. Mr. Baldwin,
Gilbert Hulse,
Isaiah Vail,
Jacob Dunning,
Elihu Slawson,
Ichabod Genung.
John Carmichal,
John Duryea.
John Sears,
Matthew Faulkner.
Oliver Hawkins,
Neil McLaughlin,
Enos Ayres.
Isaac Williams,
James Boak,
Henry Pitts,
Stephen Harlow,
John McVey,
James Brown,
Levi Miller,

William Conner.

GALLERY.

David Moore,
Annanias McCarter,
Elijah Seely,

Jonathan Hawkins,
George W. Vail,
Samuel Mills.

Jason Corwin,
Jas. McWhorter,
Peter Puff, 3rd.
Isaac Slaughter,
Wm. J. Bush,
William Faulkner.
John Gale,

Silas Pierson,
William Moore,
Joseph Bailey,
Josiah Crane,
Abraham Crane,
Stephen Crane,
Jeremiah Coleman,

William Hurtin.

List of Elders.

ᕙᗜᕗ

John White	Ordained	1804	Died	1839.
David Arnell	"	1804	"	1825.
George Houston	"	1804	"	1826.
Ephraim Everett	"	1804	"	1825.
Adam Millspaugh	"	1804	"	1824.
Enos Ayres	"	1804	"	1828.
Stephen Harlow	"	1825	"	1854.
James Boak	"	1825	"	1851.
Samuel Millspaugh	"	1825	"	1867.
John McWilliams	"	1827	"	1850.
Jason Corwin	"	1827	"	1860.
Joshua Hornbeck	"	1840	"	1857.
Joseph Slaughter	"	1851	"	1873.
James McWilliams	"	1851	"	1887.
Archibald Slaughter	"	1859	"	1867.
Stephen Harlow	"	1859	"	1887.
Charles Connor	"	1859	"	1888.
Alanson Slaughter	"	1870	"	1884.
Morris Lee	"	1870	"	1887.
Gilbert B. Corwin	"	1870	"	1889.
George Wallace	"	1870 [not active after 1885.]		
Theodore Comfort	"	1889		
David B. Myers	"	1889		
Wm. H. Puff	"	1891		
Eugene Smith	"	1891		

Necrology.

❧●❧

The following members of the Church have died during the present pastorate:

1895. March 10th, John W. Harlow, aged 73 years.
" May 4th, David Houston, aged 89 years.
" Aug. 18th, Melinda Boak, aged 82 years.
" Nov. 24th, Gussie Ferguson, aged 27 years.
1896. Feb. 8th, Maud Kelly, aged 25 years.
" April 9th, Benj. Sherwood, aged 84 years.
" April 28th, Edwin Mills, aged 70 years.
" April 28th, Mary Ann White, aged 76 years.
" May 12th, Emma Hulse, aged 55 years.
" June 7th, Daniel Clark, aged 72 years.
1895. Oct. 8th, Mrs. James McMonagle, a member of the Goodwill Church.

LIST OF OTHER DEATHS.

1895. February 2d, Mr. Samuel Armstrong.
" March 11th, Mrs. Charity Hulse, aged 88 years.
1896. March 30th, Child of Mr. and Mrs. Frank Mills.
" May 6th, Mrs. Jerdon Bull, aged 82 years.
" June 14th, George Scott, aged 35 years.
1895. June 8th, Mrs. Skinner.
" June 22d, Mrs. John Smidt.
" Nov. 8th, Harriette Alden Thompson, aged 4 years.

Present Organization,
June 1896.

ᑫ●ᑐ

PASTOR:

JAMES R. MANN.

CHURCH SESSION:

JAMES R. MANN, Moderator.

RULING ELDERS:

THEODORE COMFORT,   WILLIAM H. PUFF,
DAVID B. MYERS,   EUGENE SMITH.

The annual meeting of Session is held as near the first of April as is practicable.

Quarterly Meetings are held on the Saturday of Preparatory Service.

"Let the Elders that rule well be counted worthy of double honor, especially they who labor in the word and doctrine." 1 Tim. 5:17.

Board of Trustees.

1. The annual meeting of the board is held on the 15th day of October.

2. The annual meeting of the congregation is held on the 15th day of October.

3. The Trustees have charge of all the church property.

4. Trustees are elected to serve for a term of three years, two Trustees being elected at each annual meeting of the congregation.

34

Sabbath and Sacramental Services.

◖◖●◗◗

"Remember the Sabbath Day to keep it Holy." Ex. 20 : 8.

Public Worship—11 A. M. and 7:45 P. M.

The Lord's Supper is observed on the first Sabbath in March, June, September and December.

The Sabbath School, William H. Puff, Superintendent, is held at 10 A. M., before the morning service.

The Preparatory Service is held on the Saturday preceeding the Sabbath, on which the Sacrament of the Lord's Supper is administered, at 2 P. M.

In connection with this service the Sacrament of Baptism is observed.

Prayer Meetings and Societies.

1. The general congregation prayer meeting is held every Wednesday evening at 7:30 o'clock.

2. The Christian Endeavor prayer meeting is held every Sabbath evening at 7 o'clock.

"And they continued stedfastly in the apostles doctrine and fellowship, and in breaking of bread, and in prayers." Acts 2: 42.

"For where two or three are gathered in My name, there am I in the midst of them." Matt. 18: 20.

Christian Endeavor Society.

The Society of Christian Endeavor of the Presbyterian Church of Scotchtown was organized Sept. 30, 1889.

ACTIVE MEMBERSHIP PLEDGE.

Trusting in the Lord Jesus Christ for strength, I promise Him that I will stive to do whatever He would like to have me do; that I will pray to Him and read the Bible every day, and that, just as far as I know how, throughout my whole life, I will endeavor to lead a Christian life. As an Active Member, I promise to be true to all my duties, to be present at and take some part, aside from singing, in every meeting, unless hindered by some reason which I can conscientiously give to my Lord and Master Jesus Christ.

If obliged to be absent from the consecration meeting, I will, if possible, send an excuse for abscence to the Society.

The names of the officers, 1896, are:

President: Mrs. William H. Puff.
Vice-President: Miss Edna Slaughter.
Recording Secretary: Miss Ina Mills.
Cor. Secretary: Mr. Wellington Connor.
Treasurer: Mr. William H. Puff.

Woman's Missionary Society.

The Woman's Missionary Society of the Scotchtown
Presbyterian Church, was re-organized October 24th,
1895.

OBJECT OF THE SOCIETY.

The object of this Society shall be to impart missionary
intelligence, and to aid in the benevolent work of the
church, both in the Home and foreign field.   Art. II.

And he said unto them:

"Go ye into all the world, and preach the gospel to every crea-
ture. He that believeth and is baptized shall be saved : but he that
believeth not, shall be damned."   Mark 16 : 15-16.

OFFICERS OF THE SOCIETY.

President:	Mrs. J. R. Mann.
Vice-Presidents:	Mrs. Wm. H. Puff, Mrs. Theodore Comfort.
Recording Secretary:	Miss Edna Slaughter.
Corresponding Secretary:	Miss Bertha Mills.
Treasurer:	Mrs. Edwin Boak.

Any one can become a member of this Society by pay-
ing ten cents a month.   Art. V.

Honorary members may be received by the payment
of one dollar.   Art. VII.

Roll of Church Membership.

Mr. J. Edwin Boak,
Mrs. J. E. Boak,
Jane H. Brown,
George Brown,
Joel Brown,
Mrs. Joel Brown.
Mrs. Mary Jane Brown,
Charles M. Brinkerhoff,
Mrs. C. M. Brinkerhoff,
Jesse Bull.
Mrs. Jesse Bull.
Sarah Ester Bull,
Minnie C. Blivin,
Mrs. D. R. Clark,
Nancy Jane Comfort,
Theodore Comfort.
Mrs. Theodore Comfort,
Wellington Connor,
Mrs. W. Connor,
Minnie Courtwright,
Andrew Crans,
Mrs. Andrew Crans,
Walter Ford Crans,
Mrs. W. F. Crans.
Mrs. Jeptha Crans.
Mrs. Ada Crans,
F. Beattie Crans,
Mrs. Wm. Clark.
Mrs. Anna M. Crawford,
John F. Davis,
Mrs. Delia Davis,
Mary J. Davis,
Wm. B. Dusenbury,
Mrs. W. B. Dusenbury,
Julia Dolan,
Mrs. Mary E. Dunham,

Miss I. J. Dunham,
Irwin Dunham,
Mrs. Matilda Dunham,
Melissa Davy,
Marietta Davy,
Mrs. Eliz. Ferguson,
Frances M. Ferguson,
Mary Ferguson,
Sarah Ann Ferguson.
Emmet Goldsmith,
Mrs. E. Goldsmith,
Mrs. Carrie E. Green,
John S. Hatch,
Nancy Hatch,
Ester J. Hatch,
Jas. H. Harlow,
Chas. W. Harlow,
Mrs. C. W. Harlow,
Mabel Harlow.
Mrs. Mary B. Harlow,
Edna Beattie Harlow.
Mary Burns Harlow,
Jas. Houston,
Mrs. Jas. Houston,
Mary W. Houston,
Mrs. George Houston.
Mr. E. Helms.
Sarah Jump,
Mary Jump,
Alexander Kelly,
Mrs. Alexander Kelly.
Elija J. Kelly,
Agnes Kelly,
Kate Gertrude Kelly,
Cora A. Kelly,
Sarah M. Kelly,

Lucy Kipp,
Sarah Lindeman,
Catherine Lybolt,
Mrs. Ezra LaRue,
David Livingston,
Mrs. D. Livingston,
Jennie A. Livingston,
Mary C. Livingston,
Mrs. Frank McWilliams,
Mrs. Charlotte D. Mackinson.
Harriet Mackinson,
Mrs. Edwin Mills,
Bertha Mills,
J. D. Mills,
Mrs. J. D. Mills,
Mrs. Louisa Mills,
Ina Mills,
Jas. Edwin Miller,
Fannie Miller,
Charlotte P. Miller,
David B. Myers,
Mrs. D. B. Myers,
Mrs. J. R. Mann,
Mrs. George Miller,
Wm. H. Puff,
Mrs. W. H. Puff,
Jessie Puff,
Willliam Puff,
Mrs. Hanna Puff,
Anna F. Parsons,
Isabella B. Patterson,
Harvey Roe,
Mrs. Harvey Roe.
Mrs. Catherine Roe.
David B. Scott,
Mrs. Mary Sinsebaugh,
Anna Sinsebaugh,
Egbert Sherwood,
Egbert Sherwood, Jr.

Mrs. Albert Sherwood,
Alexander Sloat,
Mrs. A. Sloat,
Emmet Sloat,
Mary Sloat,
Mrs. Mary Ann Slaughter,
Samuel Slaughter,
Mrs. S. Slaughter,
Eugene W. Slaughter,
Edna Slaughter,
A. Amelia Slaughter,
Enos. M. Smith,
Mrs. E. M. Smith,
Emma Smith,
Mary Smith,
Ida Bell Smith,
Eugene Smith,
Mrs. Eugene Smith,
Mrs. Mary Stage,
Mary E. Stage,
Gregory Stage,
Mrs. G. Stage,
Mabel Stage,
Evelyn Sutliff,
Dr. A. C. Santee,
Mrs. A. C. Santee,
Mrs. B. C. Wallace,
Mrs. Susan Wallace.
Clara White,
Sarah E. White,
Mrs. J. H. White,
Mrs. E. Matilda Wilbur.
S. Crawford Wilbur.
Carrie Wilbur,
Sarah Wilbur,
Nellie Wilbur,
Perl Wilbur,
Mrs. Joseph Wilkins,
Oceanna Woodruff.

List of Members Dismissed During The Present Pastorate.

Mary Burns,
S. Alice Connor,
Mrs. Ellen H. Crawford,
Julia Rose McWilliams,
Minnie McWilliams
Elizabeth McWilliams,
Julia B. McWilliams,

Mrs. G. Corwin,
John Patterson,
Mrs. John Patterson,
John W. Wallace,
Emma Manse,
Mrs. Emma Helms,
Lucinda Jane Jump.

Legacies of The Church.

Received September 1890, from J. W. Corwin, Executor, three thousand five hundred and sixty-seven ($3,-567.61) dollars and sixty-one cents. Legacy from the estate of Mrs. Susan Harlow, to the Trustees of the Presbyterian Church of Scotchtown. The interest to be used in keeping the Church property in repair.

Received February 13th, 1893, from W. E. McWilliams, Executor, one thousand ($1,000) dollars. Legacy from the estate of Mrs. Margaret Coleman, to the Trustees of the Presbyterian Church of Scotchtown, without any restrictions as to the use of interest.

www.ingramcontent.com/pod-product-compliance
Lightning Source LLC
Chambersburg PA
CBHW031817090426
42739CB00008B/1316